Pitching for the Apostates

Pitching for the Apostates

Poems by

Paul Hostovsky

© 2023 Paul Hostovsky. All rights reserved.
This material may not be reproduced in any form, published,
reprinted, recorded, performed, broadcast,
rewritten or redistributed without
the explicit permission of Paul Hostovsky.
All such actions are strictly prohibited by law.

Cover art by Paul René Gauguin
Cover design by Shay Culligan

ISBN: 978-1-63980-457-3

Kelsay Books
502 South 1040 East, A-119
American Fork, Utah 84003
Kelsaybooks.com

For Marlene

Acknowledgments

Thanks to the following magazines in which these poems, sometimes in earlier versions, first appeared.

Abandoned Mine: "Do," "Literacy"
Aji: "Revision"
Baseball Bard: "True Love"
Beaver: "Cocksure"
Big Windows Review: "Bess"
Blueline: "Fishing Vest"
B O D Y: "Bicycles"
CCAR Journal: "Dear Mom," "Pitching for the Apostates"
Cerasus: "Porn"
Comstock Review: "Hiscock Park," "Playing Doctor"
Creosote: "Good Reading"
Diode: "Affiliation," "Forsythia"
Freshwater Review: "Jacob and Esau"
Havik: "Strip Tease at the Ars Poetica"
Heimat Review: "Poem for Willy Silber"
Hidden Peak Press: "Quits"
Hot Pink: "Forty Years Ago," "Wanker"
Ilanot Review: "Landmark," "The Story of the World"
I-70 Review: "Flags," "Truculent"
Jersey Devil Press: "Colander"
Literary Bohemian: "Fondly"
Mad Swirl: "Youth and Beauty"
Meditating Cat Zine: "Latifundia"
Mid-Level Management Literary Magazine: "Selfish"
Months to Years: "Snapshot"
OffCourse Literary Journal: "Good Reading," "My Grandmother's Double-U's"
One Art: "Interesting"
Only Poems: "Old Basketball Hoop"
Poetry East: "Writer," "Homegoing," "Little Hill," "Sleep by Howard"

Pulse & Echo: "Instructions for His Next Love Poem," "Osip"
Quibble: "Strength"
Scapegoat Review: "Wilkinson Swords"
SLAB: "The Curiosity Factor"
Southern Florida Poetry Journal: "His Last Poem," "Nightmare"
Star 82 Review: "Now and Then," "Prison Poetry Reading"
Subnivean: "Worship"
Taint, Taint, Taint: "Hotel Brecht," "After Fatal Mauling, Officials Find and Shoot Grizzly"
THAT Literary Review: "Coffee with the Ex," "To My 8th Grade Typing Teacher"
TheIR: "Best Listener"
Universal Table: "The Hurt Itself,"
Untenured: "Those Meetings"
TERSE: "Flight"
The Waiting Room: "Third Alternate"
Whimsical Poet: "Taking Off Walt Whitman's Clothes"
The Woven Tale: "Commandment," "Throwing the Books Away"
Young Ravens Review: "Howard in Heaven," "Letters from Camp"

Contents

I.

Bicycles	15
Forsythia	16
Writer	18
The Story of the World	19
Homegoing	20
Bess	22
Cocksure	23
Playing Doctor	24
Fondly	25
Literacy	27
Sleep by Howard	28
Prison Poetry Reading	29
Throwing the Books Away	30
Interesting	32
Colander	34
Wilkinson Swords	35
Snapshot	36
Now and Then	38
Forty Years Ago	39
True Love	40
Little Hill	41

II.

Commandment	45
Coffee with the Ex	46
Pitching for the Apostates	48
Osip	49
Flags	50
Truculent	51
Letters from Camp	52

Revision	53
Good Reading	54
Good Writing	55
Taking Off Walt Whitman's Clothes	56
Striptease at the Ars Poetica	58
To My 8th Grade Typing Teacher	60
Youth and Beauty	62
Jacob and Esau	64
Poem for Willy Silber	66
Dear Mom	68
Best Listener	69
Hotel Brecht	70
My Grandmother's Double-U's	71
Flight	73
Howard in Heaven	74

III.

Instructions for His Next Love Poem	77
Do	78
Fishing Vest	79
Selfish	80
Quits	82
Those Meetings	83
Strength	84
Porn	85
The Hurt Itself	86
The Curiosity Factor	88
Nightmare	89
Hiscock Park	91
Wanker	92
Worship	93
Latifundia	94

After Fatal Mauling, Officials Find and Shoot __Grizzly	95
Affiliation	96
Third Alternate	98
Bad Poetry Citizen	99
Old Basketball Hoop	100
Home	101
Landmark	102
His Last Poem	104

I.

Bicycles

Now I would rather remember life than live it.
I would rather imagine life than live it.
I would rather watch life going on from the sidelines
in a comfortable chair than stand in the midst of life
living it. And maybe that strikes you as sad
or perverse. And maybe I'm kind of a perv because
I'd rather watch some young people making love
than make love myself. And I would rather
read a poem about bicycles than ride a bicycle—I am done
riding bicycles. I am done making love. I am,
sadly, too old for that shit now. But I will never
be too old for the memory, or the thought, or the idea
of making love. Or the word *bicycles,* which is
as good a word as any, and better than most. In fact,
I want *bicycles* to be my last word, my dying word—
not *I love you,* or *bless you,* or *God forgive me,*
but *bicycles.* And the people standing over me—
if there are any people standing over me at the last—
will look at each other and ask if they heard me right—
"Did he say *bicycles?*" "Yes, it sounded like *bicycles*"—
as I lie on my deathbed remembering or imagining
riding our bicycles in a summer rain, then abandoning them
on the edge of a wheat field, and taking off all our clothes
because it was raining and we were already soaked
and hot and young and sweating—and running
naked through that field in the rain, and then, breathless,
sinking down in the field and making love. I don't
want to *be* in the field, in the rain, with the bugs and spiders
and rodents, the roots and stalks digging into my skin,
the itchy stems and leaves, a rat snake slithering past
and me freaking out and losing my erection—I just
want to remember or imagine those two overturned bicycles
abandoned on the edge of a field, in which we were young
and soaked and happy and making love, kickstands
pointing randomly up toward heaven.

Forsythia

Every year around this time
I think of that little boy
with the bright yellow hair

in that book my mother loved,
because she loved everything French,
and wanted me to love it, too. That book

was harder than it looked,
even in English. "What must I do,
to tame you?" asked the little prince,

a boy with yellow hair
who loved a flower, a flower a sheep
might eat if he didn't get home soon. And then

he was gone. My mother's
birthday was just last week, early spring, still cold,
some snow on the ground, that time when suddenly,

impossibly, there's yellow again: the yellowest
yellow there ever was. And then
in a few weeks it's gone. Or just

changed. Not yellow anymore but
green now, just like all the other green.
She's been dead for thirty years

and it was thirty years before that
when she first read that book to me aloud
before I could even read. I looked

at the pictures: a boy with yellow hair
and questions spilling out all over. A hat
that was really an elephant

inside a snake. And an ending
that was very sad, though he didn't die
exactly. He went home.

He loved a flower,
which made that flower unique
among all flowers.

Writer

I carry a pen
in my shirt pocket

mostly it's just
a pen in a shirt pocket

but once in a while
it leaks through

and makes an indelible
mark over my heart

and when that happens
people are moved

to put their hands
over their own hearts

and exclaim that my pen
actually had them believing

if only for a moment
that it was a matter

of life and death

The Story of the World

Praise the im-
provised, the im-
perfect, the jerry-
rigged, the jerry-
built, praise Jerry, who-
ever he was, a lands-
man after my own inept
broken heart,
which I keep trying to fix
with a little duct tape
and Elmer's glue.
Praise Elmer, praise
the tacky, tottering half-
assed job, the un-
professional, the un-
reliable, the un-
stable and unsound. Praise
all the safety pins
and paper clips
and staples holding the story
of the world together,
a story that doesn't hold up,
with its impossible plot
and vast cast of rickety
flawed characters,
every last one of us un-
believable.

Homegoing

And what if dying is like
that time I got out of school early
because I had an appointment
and I pushed open the heavy doors
and walked out into the day
and it was a beautiful spring day
or a late winter day that smelled like spring
and if it was fall it was early fall
when it's all but technically summer
and there was a whole world going on out there
and it had been going on out there the whole time
that I was stuck inside with time
and teachers and rules and equations and parsed sentences
but now here I was among the tribe
of the free and I could go this way or I could go that way
or I could just sit down right here on this bench
and look around at all the freedom
that was mine and also the work crew's
breaking for lunch beneath their ladders and also the woman's
pushing her stroller along the sidewalk and also the man's
walking his small dog and smoking a cigarette
and it belonged to the cars whooshing by with a sound like
the wind in the trees and the wind in my hair
and the wind all around me and inside me
and also above me chasing the clouds running free
and suddenly there was my mother
looking somehow a little different
in all her freedom and all my freedom
until she rolled down her window and waved
to come—now—hurry
because I had an appointment
which felt like a real buzzkill

and I briefly considered turning around
and walking away from her
and going off on my own somewhere
to be alone and free for a little longer
or maybe for forever
but then I realized there was nowhere for me to go
except home

Bess

She was wearing a white button-down shirt
with snap buttons, waiting for me
to unsnap them. But I was shy and she was
in the driver's seat. So she started unsnapping them
herself. She was 18 and had her own car already,
an old-fashioned Volvo named Bess. She had named it Bess
because Bess was an old-fashioned name. I was barely 16
and didn't have my permit yet, but I had permission
as far as the snaps. We were parked in Bess with the lights off
idling in a green place somewhere in the twilight
of my childhood. Its real name was the Volvo Amazon,
derived from the female warriors of Greek mythology.
But I don't think I knew that yet. And I don't think I knew
she wasn't wearing a bra. She'd already unsnapped
2 buttons, to show me how it was done and to show me
the little hollow between her breasts called cleavage,
an old-fashioned word that somehow also applied
to my busty grandmother living in Florida. I gingerly
unsnapped the third button. Someone inhaled audibly. Maybe me.
It felt like unwrapping a present that I'd only seen advertised
in magazines. Suddenly she unsnapped all the buttons,
impatiently ripping the wrapping paper right off.
"Thank you," I whispered gratefully, then just sat there
staring stupidly. Bess made a ticking sound
that filled the silence. It could have been
the spark plugs—you're supposed to replace them
every 100,000 miles or so. Or it could have been
the oil was low, or the valves were maladjusted,
or the drive pulleys were worn out. What did I know about
what was going on inside of Bess, in that moment,
16 years old, stupidly staring, something like time, ticking.

Cocksure

I haven't been sure of my cock since that day
it refused to stand up when it was supposed to—
which was the day we were scheduled to "do it"
one truant spring afternoon in my father's house
when I was 16 and Faith was 18 and naked
and cocksure and straddling me on the bed, whispering
"fuck me, fuck me." I'm not exactly sure why
it wouldn't stand up. It may have had something to do
with the age differential, or the vertical differential,
or the breathy imperative coming down from on high,
or the several weightinesses: There was the weightiness
of Faith herself, who wasn't twiggy, chafing and bobbing
on top of me; and the weightiness of the prospect
of losing my virginity; and the weightiness of her position
as the editor of the literary magazine vis-à-vis my position
as the diffident young poet whose exquisite death poem
had blown her and the entire literary magazine staff away
with its lively metaphors and imagery and weightiness,
which I borrowed from the weightiness of the dying
of my father, from colon cancer, only two months before.
It was his poem and it was his death. And the bed was
his bed—he had moved out of my parents' bedroom
when the pain got so bad he had to be alone—on which
Faith was alternately declaiming lines from my poem
and breathlessly adding the refrain "fuck me, fuck me"
while I lay beneath her, cock soft, in my father's
sickbed, dying to fuck her, unable to, wanting to die.

Playing Doctor

As a child, I liked playing the patient.
It felt good to be touched,
examined, puzzled over, those eyebrows
coming together over my

underlying condition. As an adult,
I liked playing the doctor, saying
to take off this, take off that, getting
to the bottom of it. Getting inside of it.

And now that I'm dying, which is taking
much longer than playing doctor ever did,
and the doctor looks young enough to be
playing doctor, holding the stethoscope

to my skin, saying to take a few
deep breaths—I'm still playing along,
pretending that the doctor can cure me,
which we both know the doctor can't,

and pretending we'll switch soon, so I can
slip my hand under the doctor's shirt
and touch the doctor's skin, which
we both know I can't. But here's what

the doctor doesn't know: playing doctor
with the doctor somehow makes me feel more alive,
especially now that I'm dying, now that it's all
so serious and no one is playing. "You can

breathe normal now," says the doc. So I eyeball
the silver stethoscope, the iconic white coat,
the clipboard on which I would write
something beautiful and life-saving

if my turn ever came.

Fondly

I remember my illness fondly
as a time when my illusions
about just about everything
were gently set aside, the way
the nurse's aide gently set aside my reading glasses
and the book I was trying to read in spite of
the pain—putting them just over there on the table
out of the way of what was more important just then,
which was the undeniable fact
that I needed to be washed. For I hadn't
washed in several days, married as I was
to the bed, the commode, the drainage tube,
and the pain. Yes, I was married
to the pain, which had a distinct element of monogamy—
it refused to share my attention
with anyone or anything, not even
with other pain. But finally the bed bath
got my attention: the nurse's aide gently
lifting my hospital gown—an indignity,
a humiliation at first—as I lay there helpless
and pale and naked, the soapy wet
washcloth sliding across my chest and belly
and genitals, my thighs and calves. And when it got to
my feet, taking each of my toes one at a time
with an almost this-little-piggy tenderness,
that's when my resistance melted away
and in its place an acceptance and a warm gratitude
gripped me so tightly that I couldn't stop whispering
the little choked thank-yous and bless-yous
escaping like too much air or too much
love from my dry, constricted throat, which was
still sore from the breathing tube. Slippery

though they are, I have tried to hold on to that acceptance
and that gratitude, which came from or were part of
my illness, which I no longer have but remember
fondly, now that I am well.

Literacy

The roofer is not a good communicator.
He doesn't tell me when he's coming.
He misspells *debris* (leaving off the *s*)
on the handwritten estimate he gives me.
He does not inspire confidence.

But the roof turns out beautiful, the debris
gets cleared away, and the house
with its new chapeau never looked so
sophisticated. His sign, *Kilraine & Son Roofing*,
in a corner of my front yard like a signature,

topples in the wind. So I put it back
facing the house. He pulls up in his pickup,
shakes his head and repositions the sign
perpendicular to the house. So people
driving by can see it. Duh. And read it.

Sleep by Howard

My cat Howard
is good at sleeping.
He can sleep on the floor.
He can sleep on the table.
He can sleep in a chair on a pile
of poems. Right now
he's sleeping in the box
my publisher sent
with ten author copies in it.
When I took them out
he climbed right in
and went to sleep.
The box is small because
the books are skinny.
And so are the poems.
He wouldn't fit if he didn't
compress himself.
Poetry is compression
and Howard is a poem
filling a boxy form,
his long complicated tail
reaching around to his head,
the last line giving a nod
to the first, the poem
tidy, circular, compressed,
yet wild, leaping, carnivorous,
its sleep delicious.

Prison Poetry Reading

When we arrived
they took our shoelaces.
But they gave them back
after the reading. Something about
weaponizing shoelaces. Nothing
about weaponizing poetry.
An inmate played the violin
as we filed in and took our seats,
then one by one we read our poems
to the inmates and the inmates
read their poems to us. You could
tell the guards didn't like poetry.
The poetry was a kind of
punishment for the guards,
a kind of escape for the inmates
who walked right out of there
in the poems, barefoot and twirling
the shoelaces, skipping and holding hands
with the guards, telling the truth,
not the whole truth but
lots of tricky emotional truths
which you can only
imagine.

Throwing the Books Away

"They smell like mildew," she said.
"That's the smell of great literature,"
I said. "I read these in college—my parents
read them, too." And I reached for a book
by Melville that I'd never actually read but
always meant to, opened it up and took a whiff.
"They smell like your parents," she said,
"who are dead and moldering, too. Let them go."
"You're killing me," I said, and dragged a forefinger
across the spines of several metaphysical poets.
"No," she said, "the mold and the mildew and the booklice
are killing you. I'm trying to save you."

So I packed them up in some large bins
and threw my back out trying to lift them
into the hatchback, which, let me tell you, hurt
less than when the used bookseller told me
he wouldn't buy any of them, couldn't sell them,
didn't want them. Then I tried giving them away
to the library, high school, Boy Scouts, YMCA,
but no takers. So I left them in the hatchback
and drove around with them for weeks, their dead
weight shifting this way and that like so many
dead poets tied up in the trunk. Soon the car reeked
of great literature. I developed a cough,
a nasty postnasal drip, and a rash that wouldn't
resolve itself. So I took them to the transfer station

and the single-stream recycling receptacles.
"We don't recycle books," said the recycling guy.
"But these are some great books by some great writers,"
I said. "OK," he said, "if you remove the bindings and glue,
and rip all the pages out, I can let you leave them here."

For well over an hour, dear reader, I ripped the hair
and guts out of greatness, and it felt like a desecration,
destroying those books just to find a place for them
in the world. But as the words of the towering dead
mixed with the things of this world—junk mail, milk jugs,
old calendars, pizza boxes, cat food tins, and all manner of
indispensable details—I began to feel, inexplicably, better.

Interesting

"Interesting," says my wife's ex-husband
to himself ("He can fix anything,"
she likes to say. "Except for his broken
marriage," I like to say.) as he considers

the door jamb, the strike plate, the lock bolt
on the door he's installing in our kitchen
because, interestingly, we all get along now
and I actually like the guy, so I hired him

to do some carpentry. Because I can barely
open a door, much less install one.
"Interesting," he says again and I know
it means he's encountered a problem—something

isn't fitting, isn't level, isn't plumb. I'm sitting
in the room across the hall with the door open, writing,
wondering about the difference between
level and *plumb*. And also, come to think of it,

between him and me. I want to say "interesting"
the way he does. But what I usually end up saying
is "shit," or "fuck," or "I give up." I'm always
closing doors, it seems, either because I'm unable

or unwilling, or, worst of all, uninterested.
But he says "interesting" to himself, and that's
interesting to me. It means he's open
to what's in front of him. Like opening a door

and walking right on through while looking
up and down and all around with interest,
willingness, maybe even amazement, something
I would like to do but never seem to do

in life—I only do it in my writing. And the fact
that my wife left a man who can fix anything,
a man who stands at the threshold saying "interesting,"
for a man who prefers to sit and write about life

than live it—that never ceases to amaze me.

Colander

Yesterday I couldn't remember the word *colander,*
a word I love and have always thought of
as one of those words that's lovelier than the thing
itself. I was holding the thing itself in my hands,
the steaming angel hair pasta draining in the sink,
when I looked at the colander and thought to myself,
"What is the name of this thing?" And maybe it's age,
and maybe it's the beginning of something more
pernicious, but in the end we have to let go
of everything. We have to let go of every single
thing and its name. And because I have always loved
the names of things more than the things themselves
I stood at the sink missing *colander,* loving it more
than the colander, more than the angel hair pasta
that I chewed abstractedly over dinner, trying to locate
colander in my mouth, where it used to live
until it disappeared—its three slippery syllables like
three spaghetti noodles in a pot of fungible spaghetti noodles.
And today, when I finally remembered it—found it right
where I'd left it—I whispered it to myself over and over
like a lover whispering the name of a lost beloved
who returns, but is untrue, and will disappear again.

Wilkinson Swords

Neither of us shaved yet—
we were just seven and five,
watching TV, when he said,
"I have to pee." And I said,
"I have to pee, too," because
I did, and because I did everything
he did, because he was older
and wiser, and a little taller.

We stood on either side
of the toilet, our tinkling streams
crossing. "Wilkinson swords!" he exclaimed,
an allusion to the crossed swords
in the TV commercial for men's razors.
We'd seen it a hundred times
because we watched a lot of TV.
I may or may not have gotten
the connection between the swords and the idea
of a close shave. But I got the connection
between the crossed swords
and the crossed streams. As sharp

as if it were today, that image
of the two of us peeing collaboratively,
seven and five, respectively,

laughing together at the bon mot,
aiming our little weenies into the toilet bowl,
artfully directing the flow
across space, across time, across
a whole lifetime of big and little ideas.

Snapshot

I am now one year older
than my mother
when she died.

And I am one year younger
than my father when he died.
So I'm right between them

like in that family snapshot
of the three of us (there were
only three of us), me in the middle,

my father leaning in, whispering
in my ear, my mother
overhearing, all of us smiling.

Except that I'm lying down now
in this hospital bed with
something that could be

anything. I don't feel well,
I say to my mother,
who knows exactly how I feel.

Then I say it to my father,
who said it often enough
when he was dying and I was

so busy living that I had no
time for his dying. And here
comes his reply, which he seems

to whisper now, but so softly
that I have to lean in very close—
and still all I can hear

are these chirping, winking, watchful
machines I'm hooked up to.
He feels so near, though,

it almost tickles—his lips grazing my ear.

Now and Then

I am in love with the past.
My past. Up to and including
this morning. This morning was lovely,
I remember it like it was
yesterday. I was sitting right here
in this chair, sipping my tea
and remembering a moment not unlike
this moment, only lovelier. A moment
from the past. Which I love more than
now. I don't love now. The Buddhists
can have now. Ram Dass and Eckhart Tolle
can have now. Give me *then*. Give me

Mnemosyne, that girl who turned up
in my middle school in the middle
of the semester with a beautiful name
no one could spell. She sat in the desk
behind me in geography class
and spun the terrestrial globe around
and around, then stopped the world turning
and told me she was from *here*—
stabbing the Peloponnesus
with a long, wormy, inky, ringed index finger.

Forty Years Ago

I've been saying "forty years ago" a lot lately.
And the twenty- and thirty-somethings
and forty-somethings are doing the math:
He must be a pretty old fucker, they're thinking,
if he can say "forty years ago" in a sentence—lots
of sentences, too many sentences—and get away with it.
But he hasn't gotten away because he's still here,
saying "forty years ago" this and "forty years ago"
that. We weren't even here forty years ago, they're
saying. But here we all are now having to listen
to this old guy going on and on about forty years ago,
like he's been there, done that, and moved on. But
he hasn't budged. "Forty years ago," he keeps saying,
and we can't keep letting him get away with that.

True Love

Maybe I loved my one
and only childhood more
than my own children's
childhoods. Maybe that's why
I kept trying to give it to them
when they were growing up themselves.
Maybe I loved my children more
as children than I love them as adults—
I don't really know them as adults.
Maybe that's unforgivable and maybe
it's untrue. Maybe what's true
is the love for that one little kid
who played center field
in the Little League game that was lost
because he misjudged a high pop or two,
and was too ashamed at the end of the inning
to go back to the dugout
and face his teammates.
So he hopped the home run fence
and walked all the way home and didn't
look back. Maybe I can't stop looking back
at that one little kid walking home
with his baseball mitt still on
like a grotesquely swollen left hand,
an affliction, an inoperable growth
I never outgrew, the tears that dried a lifetime ago
welling up anew at the drop of a hat, a ball,
a diminutive name or two
for the children I knew when they were children.

Little Hill

Look at those little kids
sledding
down that little hill,

which is just steep enough
to give them a little
speed, a little

thrill as they push off
and go flying through the world,
a world that is covered in snow

for a little while,
its sharp edges
softened.

They go up and down,
up and down that hill all day,
until they've worn it down

to the world—
grass and twigs
and brown earth poking through.

And how is it possible
that the world was able to fit
inside such a little hill?

II.

Commandment

You gotta love
all your little hatreds,
all your petty
annoyances (*annoy*
from the Latin *odium*),
for they have been
around since before Latin,
Old Italic, Etruscan,
Phoenician, Hebrew and every
other tongue—your little
hatreds have been
spitting on the earth
since the second fish
who walked on land
trod on the heels of the first,
and probably got into it
with the third fish, too.
There is such a rich
tradition of resentment,
grudge and kerfuffle—
and kerfuffle is such
a great word, you gotta
love it. You gotta love
your neighbor as yourself,
but if your neighbor is
irritating, try loving
all your irritations, try
getting in touch with
the oneness of their long
branching history, whose
latest leafy unclenching
florid blossom you are.
It's a numinous workaround
and you gotta love it.

Coffee with the Ex

We called it coffee but neither of us
had coffee. I had tea and she had
one of those flavored water drinks
in a bottle. Coffee was a euphemism,
a metaphor, an idiom for asking
the idiot who married her thirty years ago
to come sit down across from her now
and discuss the plans for the wedding—

our son's wedding. I've hated weddings
ever since ours turned out to be
a pack of pretty lies. I hadn't said more
than a few words to her since
the divorce. I had a few things
I could say now, but I didn't say them

because I've loved my son ever since
he was born. So I sipped my Earl Gray
and listened politely as she nattered on
about the bridal shower, the venue for the wedding,
the color of the bridesmaids' dresses (sage),
the menu for the rehearsal dinner
and how much it was going to cost
me. We called it coffee but neither of us

drank coffee. We called it love
but neither of us loved each other, not
really. Or maybe we did once, but it grew
tepid, cold, bitter, and the cup that runneth over
cracked, shattered, got tossed out.

"See you at the wedding," she said,
and we left the coffee shop together as the sky
opened up. Then I was sitting alone in my car,
the rain impinging on the parking lot,
thinking about myself and my old sadness—not
my son and his new happiness—feeling vaguely wrong
about just about everything.

Pitching for the Apostates

I didn't want to play for a losing team.
That was what it boiled down to.
I mean, the Jews got slaughtered,
annihilated—

everybody knew that. And as a kid
I was big into winning.
So I wanted nothing to do

with being Jewish. I stopped
going to Hebrew school. I boycotted
my own bar mitzvah.
I studied German in high school.

I married a lapsed Catholic and didn't
look back. Things went along winningly.
We celebrated Christmas and New Years.
We were Americans. We were Democrats.
We were Red Sox fans. My kids

never heard of the Four Questions
and they never asked why
I quit that team all those years ago,
though today they vaguely know
that I am still somehow vaguely

part of that team—I know it myself—
even though I don't
play for that team, don't root for that team,
wouldn't be caught dead
in the uniform.

Osip

Osip Mandelstam wrote a poem
making fun of Stalin. It got Osip
in a lot of trouble. He recited it
at a salon where it got some laughs
and then someone informed on him
and he ended up dying in a Gulag
in the Soviet Far East. I wrote a poem
making fun of Donald Trump and it got
no attention because this is America
where nobody listens to poets or reads
their poems. And maybe Osip would say
I should be grateful I live in a country
where nobody listens to poets or reads
their poems, a country where you are free
to say what you want to say, no matter
if it's false or hateful or hurtful or divisive
or throwing gasoline on the fire that
OK maybe you didn't exactly start
or exactly yell in a crowded theater,
but you're fanning the flames and it's
not only legal but politically expedient,
and all the snow in Siberia won't put it out.

Flags

I bought some stamps today.
The postal worker asked me:
"Flags, flowers, or birds?"

Not long ago it was:
"Flags, hearts, or lighthouses?"
And before that: "Flags, Earth Day or

Harlem Renaissance writers?"
I went with the writers, of course.
I never seem to choose the flags,

maybe because it's the American flag
and these days the only Americans
driving around with an American flag

flapping loudly in the wind
are the ones insisting they're the only
Americans. And I don't want to be

one of those Americans. And even though
most Americans don't write letters anymore,
I went with the birds. And also the flowers—

I bought two books of stamps because
I write a lot of letters. And even though
some birds and some flowers

are just as territorial as some Americans,
at least the birds and the flowers know
they're not the only birds, the only flowers.

Truculent

It's not that I'm
spoiling for a fight,
exactly. But I do
rehearse the fights
a lot in my head.
Fights that usually
end up not happening.
In this way I am like
my country, compulsively
upgrading my nuclear
arsenal of arguments
just in case I need them.
Truculent is today's
Webster's Word of the Day:
Eager or quick to argue
or fight. From the Latin
trux, meaning savage.
It's not that we're
savage, exactly. We do
have career diplomats,
and cultural attachés,
and poetry in translation.
And we have music,
that universal language
that soothes the savage
beast. And though we'll
likely destroy ourselves
in the final movement, still,
there will always be
this soft, gloved, refined
applause up in the balcony
where the arguments
are the opposite of savage.
They're civilized. They're
logical. They're unassailable.

Letters from Camp

I've been reading the letters I wrote to my mother
over fifty years ago from camp—she saved
them all. When she died I found them
in a shoe box in my nine-year-old hand and
voice. A hand so loopy and innocent I could
weep. A voice I know like the back
of a very small hand that used to be mine

and somehow still is. The recurring theme
is winning. ("We won the baseball game, I hit
a homer." "We won the swim meet." "We lost
the tenis tornamint because it was windy and the ball
didn't go where we hit it.") And also sugar. ("Send
more candy." "We had fribbles from Friendly's."
"Dinner was pizza and coke and desert was
choclit cake. The coke and cake were yumy.")

Winning and sugar. Sugar and winning.
And it occurs to me, though the letters stopped,
the same themes continued for fifty years: winning
at school, winning in romance, winning at work, always
the need to kill it, to destroy the competition. The sugar
that was alcohol, the sugar that was sex, the sweet taste
of every conquest. How despicable I suddenly am
to myself. Only the misspellings are endearing,
those phonetic, understandable, forgivable mistakes.

Revision

This poem is made of 100% recycled material.
All the words have been used before—there isn't
a word in this poem that you yourself haven't used.
And the spaces between the lines, and the spaces
between the words and between the letters—and even
inside of the letters—are the same perfectly breathable
open spaces that you and I have been passing through
all our lives. We are passing each other right now—
grazing each other almost imperceptibly—in the space
of this poem, occupying it at the same time for the briefest
time. Because time in this poem is from another time.
And the ideas in this poem are recycled ideas—they
flew into my head, a recycled head with curly hair and
a Jewish nose—a nose that's been recycled on Jewish faces
since the beginning of the Jewish calendar, which, by the way,
is made of 100% recycled material: all those recurring
Holy Days, daily Psalms, scrolling Torah portions to be
read aloud often. Please read this poem aloud often.
Reuse it, recycle it, share it, post it, compost it, give it
away, copy it, paste it, plagiarize it for all I care: my name
and bio will biodegrade but the poem will go on being
itself, reshaping itself, revising itself, making itself stronger.

Good Reading

When I get to the end of a book I like, I like
to go back to the beginning. Beginning
with the front matter (I like the phrase *front matter,*
its vaguely scientific ring), I like lingering
in the blurbs, then the copyright history, then right
on to the first page. The first sentence. I like to reread
that first sentence. And the second sentence.
Then the first paragraph, letting it pull me in, in
the way of currents, riptides, until I've dived
right back into the flow of the book, a book
that was so good when I got to the end I said, "God,
that was amazing, how did the writer do that?" That
is the question a good book begs. And I begin
looking for answers, finding them again and again.

Good Writing

Back when we learned how to hold our pencils,
I was the best pencil holder in class. Mrs. Morvay
said so. My pointer with its perfectly peaked knuckle
pointed downward in an excellent slope, joining
the tip of my thumb in a perfectly triangular pinch
on the leeward side of my perfectly sharpened pencil,
auguring good things to come. But good form and good
writing went the way of parchment and quills. Jon Winkels,
who sat behind me and whose pencil holding couldn't hold
a candle to mine, is a vice president now at J.P. Morgan Chase,
and Arthur Lafferty, whose pencil luffed and lurched crookedly,
sailed on to become a rich entertainment attorney at RCA,
while I'm still sitting here with my poor number 2 pencil
and good form, writing in perfect obscurity, waiting to be praised.

Taking Off Walt Whitman's Clothes

after Billy Collins

Myself,
I'm not into men but
those armpits
finer than prayer

kind of piqued
my curiosity. "I'm dead,"
he said, "so you'll have to
do the honors

yourself."
His eyes bore right into me
as I unbuttoned first one button
of his yellowed workman's shirt

and then the other buttons. It was
an overcast morning in Brooklyn,
a scent of the docks in the air,
as I guided his hairy arm

out of its long sleeve,
then raised the arm over his head
in the manner of referees
and prizefighters. A stevedore

gave us a disapproving scowl
as I grazed the nest
of his armpit with my nose. I stopped
somewhere

around there, waiting for him
to sigh or moan or
spur me on, but he was
still dead. So I undid

the father of free verse's belt buckle
and unzipped his fly
and I assumed
that what he assumed

was that I'd go all the way,
and maybe I would have if
I was a better poet.
But instead I ended the poem

too soon. I should have kept going.
It might have been different
from what I supposed,
and luckier.

Striptease at the Ars Poetica

First I took off my coat
because I was hot
and then I took off my hat
because forty percent of your body heat is lost through your head
which is a myth
but I like certain mythologies
and I like certain hat hair
which is perverse I know but I'm kind of a perv
so I took off my scarf because it was itchy
and then I took off my gloves
because it's hard to unbutton your shirt when you're wearing
    gloves
and I wanted to unbutton my shirt
so I unbuttoned my shirt
and I took it off and twirled it around over my head
and tossed it through the air
the way they do in strip joints and in movies
and at weddings
okay maybe they don't do that at weddings
they toss bouquets at weddings
and they twirl napkins at weddings
but you get the idea
and when I got the idea I took off my pants
because when a man gets aroused
he has this inexorable compulsion
to show his erection to someone who appreciates it
the way he appreciates it
as though it were something he had made
with his own hands
which some erections are
so then I stood there steeply rocking
in a sea of aloneness

because I was utterly alone in the Ars Poetica
with no one to appreciate what I had made
so I took off my shoes and my socks
and I hung my left sock on my erection
like a windsock
that shows the direction and strength of the wind
I didn't make the wind but I made a windsock
or the likeness or the image of a windsock
and I stood there naked in the wind for a brief moment
admiring what I had made
because it was beautiful and true and it slanted a little
due to the diminishing strength of my erection
and all of a sudden I felt very foolish
all of a sudden I felt very cold
and alone and with no direction
so I removed the sock and I put it back on my foot
and I put my other sock on my other foot
and I dressed quickly and self-consciously
and stuffed my hat and scarf and gloves back inside my coat
    pockets
and then with my coat in one hand and my shoes in the other
I tiptoed out of there in my stockinged feet
and I only am escaped alone to tell thee

To My 8th Grade Typing Teacher

Because I am a writer who can't write
in longhand, and because my fingers
are always itching for the keyboard, my silent
piano, and because writing, for me, has always been
more like making music anyway
than having anything to say,

I am writing to say thank you, Miss Statchel,
wherever you are, for teaching me how to type in the 8th grade,
back when I was a cross between
a suppurating pimple with sensory organs on it
and a stomach lurching queasily down a junior
high school hallway. You saved my life,

which sounds hyperbolic, I know, but hey,
as the bumper sticker says, Art Saves Lives,
and I think I can safely say
that typing is the one skill I learned in junior high
that has stood me in good stead, a phrase
that's been around since the 15th century,
which is an etymological factoid as useless
as all the facts and dates and definitions

we memorized in junior high. But I remember
your classroom, Miss Statchel, a manual typewriter bolted
to every desk, and Linda Farrell sitting demurely
in the desk next to mine. I might have
fallen in love with her if I didn't
fall in love with typing first: a quirky, QWERTY
love of all the letters, and all the words,
with lots of touching with all my fingers,
except the thumbs—the right thumb making space

while the fingers made time with the letters,
the left thumb hovering over everything, looking on. I wonder
about that left thumb, why its fate is to be forever
left out, left over, like a maiden aunt, perhaps a little
like you, Miss Statchel, lonely, rigid, watchful, chaperoning
the fingers as they make love to the letters and the words—
yet never joining in the joy of the consummation.

Youth and Beauty

When I was young and good-looking
I mean really young like thirteen or fourteen
I mean really good-looking like Leanne Simon definitely noticed
me in the halls and in the cafeteria
even though she never said a word to me
when I was young and good-looking
and she was young and good-looking
in fact Leanne Simon was probably
the best-looking girl in my grade
she was so pretty you just wanted to stare at her
and look for the flaw in her perfection
because there had to be a flaw but there was no flaw
and if she had wanted to be with me like go out with me
which of course she didn't but just for the sake of argument
I wouldn't even have known what to do with Leanne Simon
I mean I probably would have shown her my stamp collection
and my coin collection and my runner-up tennis trophy
or maybe the nutcracker my parents brought home from Denmark
with the intricately carved wooden handles
but I don't think I would have touched her because
when I was young and good-looking
I was less interested in touching beauty than just staring at it
and looking for the flaws and not finding any
so I definitely wouldn't have wanted to get in her pants
because I didn't know what was in her pants
and didn't want to know
I just wanted to be around her and in front of her
and on every side of her especially her good side
so I probably would have showed her my record collection
and maybe we would have sat on my bed together
and listened to records and not even given a thought
to what two young and good-looking people might do

on a bed or in a bed but I'd like to think
that maybe I would have asked her to dance
which is one of the best ways to be around beauty
and examine its perfection from all sides
for the flaws that aren't there
but chances are I wouldn't have had the balls to ask her to dance
as I sat there next to her on the bed listening to the music
and fidgeting with the nutcracker in my hands
after she'd held it in her hands and admired it and handed it back to
   me

Jacob and Esau

My bar mitzvah portion was the story
of Jacob and Esau and the lentil soup.
At thirteen I was as smooth as Jacob:
I had learned just enough Hebrew to read
that bit from the Torah aloud, impress the congregation
and get the money. It was all a kind of fraud—
I had no idea what any of the words *meant*.
I had never even tasted lentil soup.
And when I finally did, I didn't like it. The story
of Jacob and Esau and the lentil soup
and the blind father, Isaac, as it turns out,
is a story of fraud. And thirteen isn't the age
when manhood begins—that was the biggest fraud—
though it roughly coincides with the onset
of puberty. At thirteen I could count the number of hairs
that were growing down there: approximately
thirteen. I learned about approximate equality
in algebra class that same year: when any two quantities
are close enough in value that the difference
is negligible, you use the approximately-equal-to sign
with a squiggly, which looked like one of the curling
tender tendrils growing down there. So it all fit together
approximately. I didn't have a hairy brother like Esau
or a blind father like Isaac, but I was smooth:
practically all of my friends were hairier than me.
I knew this because of gym class and because of
peripheral vision. I pretended not to see, but I saw.
I saw I would be a late bloomer. I saw that lentil soup
was an acquired taste. I saw I wouldn't start liking it
until many years later, when I'd grown enough pubic hair
to sport an excellent beard. A beard is technically
pubic hair on your face—any hair that wasn't there

before puberty is technically pubic hair, a factoid
that I thought the rabbi might appreciate. So I told him
during one of our boring weekly bar mitzvah lessons.
He made a face like he had indigestion, then fondled
his pubic hair and told me to keep reading. Just keep reading.

Poem for Willy Silber

She was only ten, my mother
said, but you kept pursuing her
at the tender age of twelve,
Willy Silber, nice, quiet boy
whose parents owned a bakery,
or they lived above a bakery—
there was some connection
with a bakery, the smell of bread
in the oven, she said. This was
in Maastricht, in 1939, and everyone
had a bicycle. So she had a bicycle
and a boyfriend, though she didn't
call you her boyfriend because no one
else in her class had a boyfriend,
and everyone teased her about you,
and it made her feel uncomfortable,
she said. Then one day you invited her
to your bar mitzvah. And she didn't know
if she should go. She didn't want to
especially, but she didn't want
to hurt your feelings, she said. But
that never came about, she said,
because our family fled Holland—
a mad scramble on the last ship out.
The ship was called *The Statendam,*
she said. And though she didn't say
what happened to you, Willy Silber,
nice, quiet boy who stayed behind
with your family and the other Jewish families,
of course I know what happened to you,
gentle, faceless boy who loved my mother
when she was ten and you were twelve,

who invited her to your bar mitzvah,
and she would have gone, she would have,
because she didn't want to hurt your feelings.
You would have been very hurt, she said.

Dear Mom

After you died,
I found that cassette tape
of you talking about your life.
It was under a pile of letters in a shoe box
on the closet floor,
labeled *Memories* in that hand
I would know anywhere,
a hand like a kind of
face. It's the only recording
I have of your voice, your laugh, your way
of talking: I can hear you begin
to say a word, then pause, then choose
a different word—I can hear you
thinking. To think you've been dead
all these years and I can hear you thinking.
I can even hear you lip the cigarette
before you light it, still talking
with it unlit in your mouth,
lips pressed together like
a ventriloquist's. Then I hear
the match strike and flare, I hear you
inhale. Exhale. I hear you
breathing. I have listened to that tape
hundreds of times since you died.
I listened to it again just this morning.
I'm listening very closely. Much more closely
than I ever listened to you
when you lived and breathed.

Best Listener

The dog of myself
walking the dog of the dog
through the dog of the world.
I've been talking to myself
a lot lately. Too much, probably.
I am my best listener. No one
hears me out like I do.
The dog of the dog stops, pees
on a tree, and suddenly
I have to go, too. "The good
stuff, too, is contagious," I say
to the dog of myself zipping up.
The danger, of course, which is
posted on the trail—Steep Decline
Ahead—is the more you talk to yourself
the more you begin to resemble
a guy on a park bench talking to himself,
eyes wild, fly open, gesticulating
at his own inscrutable privacies,
barking at the dogs of the people
of the world passing by.

Hotel Brecht

No one is reading Bertolt Brecht
in the Brecht Hotel. Most of the guests
haven't even heard of him, though they've heard
of the famous complimentary full breakfast,
the comfortable rooms, the luxurious amenities,
and the convenient location—just a short walk
to the Theater District, the Brandenburg Gate, the Memorial
to the Murdered Jews of Europe. And there's bacon
and sausage and eggs any way you like them,
and muffins and croissants and Danish pastries,
and pancakes and waffles and a veritable cornucopia
of apples, oranges, grapefruit, watermelon,
green grapes, red grapes, concord grapes, pineapple,
cantaloupe, honeydew, strawberries, blueberries and kiwi,
a bank of coffee urns and hot water, an assortment
of teas, milk and honey, cream and sugar and an array
of sugar substitutes. As for the murdered Jews of Europe,
many of them had likely heard of Bertolt Brecht,
perhaps read one of his poems, or hummed a song
from one of his plays as they went about doing
what the living do. And though he wasn't a Jew,
he fled Nazi Germany in 1933 and didn't come back
until after the war. In his poem "Die Bücherverbrennung,"
a banished poet discovers his works are not on the list
of books to be burned by the fascist regime, and cries out:
"Burn me! I order you to burn me!" For the sake of appearances
there's a framed photograph in the eponymous hotel lobby
of the bespectacled, unsmiling Brecht—a poet and playwright
who rejected the comfortable, the convenient, the easy,
who wanted to leave his audiences hungry, and uncomfortable
with what he showed them—injustice, exploitation,
complacency—so they would be moved to go forth
and make change in the world. He didn't want them satisfied,
sated. He wanted them hungry. Uncomfortable. Burning.

My Grandmother's Double-U's

"Vee got out in de nick of time,"
says my grandmother.
Her double-u's are vees,
her tee-aitches are dees. "Dat's how
vee saved our lives." Her ar's
are tiny gargles, little swallowed drum rolls
down in her throat. I try
to help her with them, to raise them up
into her mouth. "Repeat after me, Bubbie:
I'd really rather; rrreally rrrather."
But they refuse to budge,
they're stuck down there, dug in, planted,
rooted. And because my mother was only ten
when our family fled that nightmare,
her double-u's were vees, too, back then.
"The reason I speak English now
without an accent," says my mother,
"is because the very day we arrived
Zadie announced: 'From now on
vee speak only English.' None of us
knew a word of English." "Vee knew a little
from school," corrects my grandmother.
"And *die gehorsame Tochter* I was," says my mother,
"I dutifully complied: I spoke only English
from that day forward. With an accent
for a number of years, but then the accent
disappeared." My grandmother nods,
smiles, says nothing else, keeping her vees
to herself. But her vees are "we",
her vees are us, my family, me. And the music
of those vees and tee-aitches
and drum-rolled ar's—all the variations

on that theme—whenever I hear it in the mouths
of people speaking English with foreign accents—
plays in my ears like a dirge: beautiful, foreign,
familiar. Faintly heartbreaking.

Flight

Have you noticed
that birds on the ground usually walk or hop
instead of fly?
But they will fly if you get inside their
flight initiation path,
which is just a fancy way of saying
too close for comfort.
Humans like to say things in fancy ways
that can usually be said simpler.
This is used to distance other humans.
Birds, like humans, will keep a certain distance
between one another.
If you look at birds on a wire,
if you look at humans hanging out together,
the ones with smaller spaces between them
are usually mates or offspring or really good buds.
Birds would rather walk or hop than fly because
flight takes way more energy—
you wouldn't do it if you didn't have to.
But you'll do it to escape predators,
and also when life over there is a better option
than life over here. This is called migration.
Humans would rather fly than walk, but mostly
they walk. Sometimes they walk very long distances
and when they finally arrive they are told to turn back.
The humans are told to turn back.
As if there weren't enough nesting materials to go around.
Humans have learned a lot from birds,
but we still don't fathom—(*fathom* from the Old English:
to measure with a distance of outstretched arms,
to encircle with the arms, to embrace)—
we still don't fathom flight.

Howard in Heaven

I hear licking
coming from
the bathroom.

It's my cat
Howard
in the shower
after I have

showered,
the damp
hanging there

rich as
a rainforest
after a rain,
so thick you could

drink it,
which Howard is
doing
in delicate

little sips,
licking the tiles,
nipping the droplets
clinging there

with the quick
pink arrow
of his tongue,

and it sounds
downright
delicious.

III.

Instructions for His Next Love Poem

If you write me another love poem, jeez,
keep me out of it, will you please?
And whatever you do, no mention of
my breasts. Try writing about love
instead of my lips and hair and eyes.
And keep it simple. If it simplifies
half as much as love simplified
before it got complicated, I'll have lied
if I say it isn't any good. And it'll be very
good if I can read it without a dictionary.

Do

For Dooder

"I'll do the portobello omelet
with bacon and swiss," says my son
to the waiter. And when the waiter leaves

I say, "*Do?* What happened to *have?*
You aren't going to *do* anything—
they're going to *do* it in the kitchen
for you. Then you're going to *have* it."

"Dad, the language is changing,
dude. It's alive. People say *do* now.
All my friends say it. You can say it, too."

"I will never say *do,*" I say.
And he shrugs as if to say *have
it your way.* Then he checks his phone.

"Do you have to always be doing that?" I say.
"Doing what?" he says.
"That," I say, pointing at the phone.
"Can't we have a normal conversation

the way normal people do?"
"You just said *do,* Dad. You're
such a doodad." And smiling triumphantly,
he puts his phone away. And gives me my due.

Fishing Vest

I don't like fishing.
But I like hyperbole.
It had a hundred pockets.
I saw it in the window
of the sporting goods store
and I thought: now every poem
shall have its pocket. And I thought:
let there be plenty of pens
and pocket combs, a pocket
dictionary, a box of raisins,
a pocket watch, a deck of cards,
and a pack of cigarettes.
I like a poem that can hold
numerous small swindles
and lots of harmonicas,
a childhood memory
of an imitation turd
from a novelty shop
on Hancock Street. I hadn't
smoked in years, but now
I wanted a pack of cigarettes.
And I wanted a deck of cards.
I didn't want to go fishing.
I didn't give a shit
about fishing. What I wanted
was a poem that could hold
everything. Everything I wanted
and everything I didn't want
but was dealt anyway.
I wanted those pockets.
A hundred of them.
And the one that got away.

Selfish

Bill sure hated to work.
He didn't hate his job, he just hated
to work. And then he got sick
and being sick became his job.

"Going to dialysis three days a week
sure beats going to work," he said.
"Are you serious?" I said. "You'd rather
be sick with renal disease than go to work?"
"I have every other day off," he said.
"I get disability and social security. It's a great
country. I don't do a stitch of work, I just
sit in the dialysis chair all day
and get a lot of reading done. I get to flirt with the nurses.
It's a good life."

But after eight and a half years of it,
Bill had had enough of it. His vision was going
and his knees were going and his feet
were almost gone. And he didn't want
to end up blind and in a wheelchair, he said.

"So what are you going to do?" I said.
"I'm going to stop going to dialysis," he said. "It's the perfect
suicide. It's legal. It's painless. Come on up to Schenectady
and say goodbye to me."

So I drove up to Schenectady
the day after his last day of dialysis. And I spent the long
weekend with him. Three days of gallows humor
and morphine which he got from the hospice people
just in case he needed it. He didn't need it
but he wanted to try it. And he wanted

to start smoking cigarettes again because
what the hell, he'd be dead soon anyway.
He was free to do what he wanted to do,
free to eat what he wanted to eat, and free
from the dialysis finally. He was even free from the guilt
that some of his friends and family tried to lay on him—
'selfish' they called it. But the guilt got filtered out
like the excess water and toxins the dialysis
removed when his kidneys stopped doing the job.

And now that his job was dying, "It sure beats
going to work," he said, taking a long drag
on his cigarette, coughing fitfully for a breathless
minute, then smiling at me boyishly through the tears.

Quits

Let's call it quits. Let's take
five. No, seven, in honor of
the seventh day. No, in honor
of the cigarette, which takes
exactly seven minutes to smoke
all the way down. Let's call it
a day, a week, two weeks. Let's
take a liquid lunch and not
come back for days, weeks, months.
Let's not and say we did. I used to
say that a lot as a kid: Let's not
and say we did. It sounded
subversive and anarchic. I was
big into anarchy and subversion.
I quit high school and landed on my feet
in a college for creative fuck-ups
on the Hudson. I quit marriages
and landed on my feet in other
marriages. I'm all for quitting.
Quitting gets a bad rap. The people
who tell you to never give up,
to keep fighting no matter what—
don't you just want to slap them?
A few of them are standing around
my hospital bed right now, saying
to keep fighting. I want to get up
and slap them, one by one, then
hug them, hard, then lie back down
and call it quits.

Those Meetings

Are you still going to those meetings?

Those meetings are like no meetings you've ever attended
they always start on time and end on time
and everyone introduces themselves before they speak
so that no one forgets who they are or what they are
and they don't interrupt each other or even address each other
they just go around the room and tell these stories
and the stories are true and they're all the same story
with slight variations in the precious indispensable details
and everyone thanks each other in a chorus of thank-yous
and no one takes minutes and there are no action items
because everyone's action item is the same action item
and they do it together and they do it alone and no one
checks to make sure it got done and no one checks
to see who belongs at the meetings and who doesn't belong
because everyone belongs if they say they belong
and they can't kick you out unless you're disrupting the meeting
and in that case they do it gently and invite you back
and there are morning meetings and lunchtime meetings and
nighttime meetings and beginner's meetings before the meetings
and there are no executives and there is no meeting agenda
and they take turns running the meetings which always
run smoothly and everything gets done that needed to be done
and everything gets said that needed to be said
and they'll tell you there's no such thing as a bad meeting
and if you think your meetings should run more like
those meetings if you think your work meetings or town meetings
or city meetings or state or country's meetings should run like
those meetings if you think the whole world should run more like
those meetings the people who go to those meetings won't disagree
but they won't be interested in extrapolating from those meetings
how to run the world because they're not trying to change
the world they're only trying to change their minds about the world

Strength

Step right up,
don't miss it,
a single vowel
holding up seven
consonants like
seven continents
on an invisible barbell,
three on the left,
four on the right,
the fourth one tilting
the whole thing forward,
giving it lift, giving it
that voiceless dental fricative,
that little extra oomph
we all need to keep
going in a word
in a world that goes
without saying
and all in just
one syllable.

Porn

Nose pressed to the screen
window, my cat Howard

is looking at the sparrows
in the hedge, his mouth

twitching with desire,
his claws

extending, retracting, the whole
of his attention

taut, poised, pointing
at all the winged

bodies coming
and going.

The Hurt Itself

There was no one to blame
when I closed the laptop
and got up from the chair
and tripped over the cat

(who was just sitting there
quietly minding his own
ruminations in the shadow
of the chair) and fell forward

and hit my shoulder hard
against the fireplace mantle,
jamming my index finger,
and knocking over a knick knack

made of glass (which belonged
to my mother, who'd been dead
twenty-nine years). I winced
and held my aching shoulder,

and licked my smarting knuckle,
and surveyed the broken glass.
And then I looked around for
someone to blame. It wasn't

my fault that I didn't see the cat
hidden in the shadow. It wasn't
the cat's fault for being a cat
ruminating in shadow behind a chair,

and it wasn't my mother's fault
for buying a glass knick knack,
and dying, and leaving it to me.
Leave it to me, I always find

someone to blame. But this time
there was no one, there was nothing.
Which hurt more than the hurt itself
almost. And then it hurt differently

than the hurt. Then less than the hurt.
And finally, not blaming anyone
for the hurt itself didn't hurt at all.
In fact it actually felt pretty good.

The Curiosity Factor

Don't you love that it's a thing,
the wretchedness
on the other side
spilling over, puddling
like transmission fluid or
blood, forcing us to slow down
because it's all so irresistible,
so infectious that we can't
look and we can't stop looking
at the beautiful catastrophes—
beautiful for the way they
bring us together over them—
in a world where every last one of us
is stuck here with no idea why,
hoping and praying it'll all become clear
somewhere up ahead,
the unseen hands of angels
bearing brooms, bearing stretchers,
and wreckers with winches
not exactly clearing it up
but clearing it away somehow
before we ever get there,
so we never know in this lifetime
what it was we were waiting for
or the reason for our long suffering.

Nightmare

You're attending a reunion
of all the people
you've slept with in your life—
it isn't a large number,
less than legion, more
than minyan, a number
divisible only by itself and you.
It's a formal gathering in a room with
large upholstered chairs
and potted weeping figs,
a small bar in the corner
where two women you don't recognize
are seriously kissing, holding their drinks aloft
like tiny sloshing mountain lakes
in their slender raised hands. You aren't
dressed for the occasion,
you realize as you look down
at your ashy underwear and ten
poor stubby toes. It seems
you're expected to make a speech
which everyone has traveled far
through time and space to hear. You're
unprepared. No script. No notes. You
haven't even given it a thought. Now
you frantically ask one ex-lover
after another for a writing utensil. You
actually say "writing utensil" the way
your teacher said it in the 3rd grade.
No one has a pen. But someone
has an eye liner pencil. Now for
some paper. You're holding a damp
drink napkin in your hand, shaking it

in the air to dry it. If only you
could write, you think, maybe
you could still make something out of this
nightmare, something beautiful and true.

Hiscock Park

East Newton Street, Boston

I pass it sometimes on my walk from Back Bay
to the medical center, this tiny city park the size
of a brownstone at the end of a row of brownstones—
like a missing tooth at the end of a row of teeth—
filled with topiary, a crushed-rock pathway, a stone bench,
in this neighborhood with a large gay community.

And the name, emblazoned on a wrought iron gate—
Hiscock—gets me thinking: Could this be an anonymous
memorial to a lover who died young, perhaps of AIDS,
a sort of ode to his youth and beauty and the fullness
of his maleness? I imagine an older, grieving, dapper
gay man of means deciding to buy this plot, lovingly

planting it, tending it, then naming the park after
the thing itself—the younger man's perfectly torqued
tumescence, risen, swollen, exquisite and alive—
a shrine to the memory of it, to the shape of his lost
happiness, the warm pulsing place which he had loved
to worship, watch grow, take in, drinking in the love

of his ravishing lost-forever young lover. I imagine
all this, then I google "Hiscock Park" just to see what
comes up. Not surprisingly, no such story. But the name
Hiscock, as I read on my iPhone, was brought to England
after the Norman conquest in 1066. It's a diminutive form
of *Richard,* a pet name, —*cock* being a medieval term of
endearment. Which is, I like to think, a not unrelated story.

Wanker

Das Ewig-Weibliche zieht uns hinan
                    —Goethe

I don't remember much from German class.
I think *ziehen* means to pull, and I remember
pulling on myself a lot in the bathroom
while picturing Gretchen Wagonseller

who sat in the seat in front of me, her lovely
long blond hair falling eternally downward,
her breathy, faltering voice conjugating *ziehen*
for the whole class–*ich ziehe, du ziehst, er zieht*—

which gave me a boner that I couldn't very well
pull on in German class. But I pulled on it very well
once I got to the bathroom, and I went on pulling
all that semester, and also the next. After graduating

I forgot almost all of my German, but I kept on
conjugating the verb of myself in a bathroom—
many bathrooms—for years. Decades. Even after
I got married—and not to Gretchen Wagonseller—

I never graduated from the pulling, or the trying
to imagine *das Ewig-Weibliche,* the Eternal Feminine,
which I can't quite imagine and can't stop imagining—
my opus magnum. Deal with the devil indeed.

Worship

sounds like *warship*.
Sunday *warship*. Come
and *warship* with us.
And isn't that what
we end up doing, rigging
the tall ships, praying
for propitious skies,
then going off to fight
the good fight? I don't think
God wants our worship
anymore than Faith
Lubecki wanted mine
back in the 10th grade
when I was totally smitten
with the idea of her. Lord,
how I worshiped her,
gave her my adoration,
was ready to cross swords
with any and all rivals.
But she didn't want
to be worshiped and adored.
She just wanted what
everyone wants—even God:
to love and to be loved.
But the thing was, I didn't
really know how to love.
Most people don't. Faith
ended up marrying an Orthodox Jew
from Crown Heights, NY,
whom she gave a boatload
of kids. Me, I'm still learning
how to love. And how to pray.
Blessed are the slow learners.

Latifundia

All we needed was a dictionary
and our imaginations
and a few good

players. One of us
would look for a word
the others didn't know, like *latifundia,*

and one at a time we'd take turns
making up definitions
to rival the real one—

latifundia: a fungal infection of the inner ear
latifundia: a landed estate worked by slaves
latifundia: a species of salt-water marsh grass

—and then we'd vote
on the best and most plausible.
And the one that got the most votes

won. It was very democratic.
It was bullshit at its best.
Latifundia: the capital of Tanzania

Latifundia: the Latino diaspora
in Pakistan and India
Latifundia: the genus of horned ungulates

that includes the gnu.
And it was always a real coup
whenever the invented trumped the true

because that was how we knew
our bullshit was some powerful voodoo.

After Fatal Mauling, Officials Find and Shoot Grizzly

Because why?
Because she was a murderess

or because she loved her children
or because she was hungry

or because she could have killed
again? Do you ever

find yourself rooting for the wrong side?
I feel sorry for the grizzly.

She was probably frightened.
She was probably made to feel exposed

the way very tall people are made to feel exposed
standing among us. The way

last night in the dark,
standing beside the open refrigerator door,

helping myself to more cake with my fingers,
shoveling it in, chewing hummingly,

when you suddenly turned on the light,
I was made to feel.

Affiliation

I was reading this cat research—
new research about cats—
that said we don't really know cats;
there are 58 million pet cats in America
and we don't really know them.

It said they don't like their cat food bowl
near their water bowl. Who knew?
So I moved my cat's water bowl
into the other room. He looked
nonplussed, then rubbed up against my leg
and gave my shin a headbutt.

Previous cat researchers, said this cat researcher,
have hypothesized that cats rub up against you
to mark you with their scent. That's balderdash,
said this cat researcher. It's really their way
of affiliating. I liked the sound of that—
affiliating. I also liked the sound of *balderdash*.

Affiliate comes from the Latin
'to adopt a son.' *Fillius* is Latin for son.
No one knows where *balderdash* comes from.

Now when my cat rubs up against me
or gives me a headbutt,
I know he wants to affiliate. "You wanna
affiliate?" I ask him in that baby talk
that cat lovers use with their cats
that annoys everyone else including other cat lovers.

I adopted my cat from the animal shelter.
But the research isn't clear, said the cat researcher,
exactly who is adopting who, with all this affiliating
going on. 58 million and counting.

I pick him up and we affiliate. He sits in my lap,
wise and regal, keeping his own counsel
and dignity, while I babble on in baby talk.

Third Alternate

When I applied for that fellowship
I got a letter congratulating me
for being chosen "third alternate."

It went on to explain that if the one
who actually won the fellowship
couldn't make it, for whatever reason,

and if the first alternate couldn't
make it, either, and if the second
alternate couldn't make it, well then, I,

the third alternate, could have it.
Of course I never got it. But I got
that I was third alternate. I got that.

And I still get that. Not the winner
but not exactly the loser either.
Better than mediocrity but not quite

greatness. Not quite. Not even
close. Congratulations are in order—
in order. Your call is important to us,

it will be answered in the order
of excellence. (Here follows painfully
bland recorded background music.)

Bad Poetry Citizen

The only poetry readings he goes to
are his own poetry readings. And he doesn't
teach or mentor or translate or edit
or blurb. He's such a schlub.
All he does is make poems.
And he borrows without crediting.
He cheats: he double-
dips, gives his First North American Serial Rights
to any and all takers, the cad. He loves
certain poems but he dislikes
poetry. And he dislikes Marianne Moore
except for that one poem. He dislikes
poets because he sees himself in them
and doesn't like what he sees.
If you tell him you love his poems,
he loves them even more. And he loves *you*
for loving them. But if you don't love them,
he hates them. He's that suggestible.
He's a chameleon—not in the Keatsian sense,
but in the capricious, duplicitous, surreptitious sense.
And he can never remember the word
integrity. Probably because he doesn't have any.
He has no empathy either. "But his poems
are full of pathos," I hear you objecting.
That's right, they are. And Aristotle
was right, too: the poet is an imitator.
And he's a good poet, so he's a good imitator,
but he's a bad poetry citizen. He's a liar,
a thief, a cheat, and a scoundrel. Someone
really ought to call the poetry police.

Old Basketball Hoop

This abandoned post
on the edge of the driveway,
holding up the backboard and the rim
for more than twenty years now
in the same rusted pose,
like a monument to my children's
childhoods, which I pass beneath
every day on my way to work,
this memorial to H-O-R-S-E,
and Around the World,
and *nothing-but-net,*
a metal net that went ka-ching,
a sound so rich and gratifying
whenever we scored a basket,
and it still tinkles softly
when the wind blows through it,
though no one has taken a shot
in years. The whole contraption
with its frozen posture
reminds me a little of myself—
still holding out, still holding up
the circle of an empty embrace
for those same children
who are done being children,
who have moved away and won't
be moving back. It's a little sad
and a little ridiculous, frankly,
that a whole sandbox of sand
that once upon a time I poured
into that hollow base—
so the whole thing wouldn't tip over—
is still sitting quietly inside
just waiting for those children
to come out and play.

Home

Whenever I hear you,
whoever you are,
tawlking like that,

saying dawg or cawfee,
or when you cawl me
Pawl, I feel a kind of

kinship with you
going all the way back to the Garden
State, where I haven't

lived since I was a boy.
Nevertheless, people tell me
they still hear it in me.

I can't hear it in me.
But I can hear it in you,
whoever you are,

and whenever I do,
it feels as if I know you
intimately, even if

I don't know you at awl.

Landmark

My mother's new house
was the third house on the left,
the one with the big rock in the front yard—
you couldn't miss it. This was
on the third rock from the sun, the one
with billions of people on it—you couldn't
leave it, not even if you died
three months after retiring and moving to Boston
to be closer to your grandchildren. It was
a nondescript rock, a boulder really,
that the builder probably decided on a lark
to leave there: a sort of lawn ornament,
a sort of landmark. Sandstone or limestone
or maybe shale. She'll have a hard time
selling it with that rock in front, said my wife.
She won't sell it, I said. She's not leaving.
She died three months later, suddenly, unexpectedly,
a bacterial infection that overwhelmed her overnight.
We never found out how she got it. There are
more bacteria living on your skin
than people living on the third rock from the sun.
My son liked to climb it when we visited.
He was only 4. His sister was 2. They don't
remember the rock and they don't remember
my mother. The buyer said he didn't like the rock
but it wasn't a dealbreaker. The two of us
stood in the front yard negotiating. I told him
it was a great landmark—you couldn't miss it.
I told him my kids liked to climb it. I told him
my mother lived here only three months—she hadn't even
hung her pictures yet. Suddenly, unexpectedly,
I started to choke up. He put his hand on my shoulder

to console me, this stranger, this buyer, a tender
gesture that only made it worse, and I began to sob
uncontrollably. I hid my face in my hands
and turned away from him. And faced the rock.

His Last Poem

It was just a tiny thing,
a handful of unrhymed couplets

about the warm tears
of old men,

tears that bless everything,
help nothing, no one—

each line like an empty clothesline
with a few orphan clothespins,

no clothes, no colors flapping
in the breeze. Just the sagging

line with its suggestion of a house
on one side, a tree on the other,

or two trees and no house—
then the clothespins flying away.

About the Author

Paul Hostovsky's poems appear and disappear simultaneously (voila!) and have recently been sighted in places where they pay you for your trouble with your own trouble doubled, and other people's troubles thrown in, which never seem to him as great as his troubles, though he tries not to compare. He has no life and spends it with his poems, trying to perfect their perfect disappearances, which is the working title of his new collection, which is looking for a publisher and for itself. He is the recipient of such rebukes as "You Never Want to Do Anything" and "All You Care About Are Your Stupid Clever Poems."

www.ingramcontent.com/pod-product-compliance
Lightning Source LLC
Chambersburg PA
CBHW022015160426
43197CB00007B/443